Contents

Correct handwriting position

Left-hander

Finger tips 4cm from tip of pencil

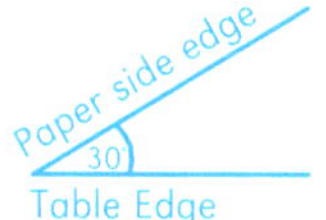

Elbows off the table

Right-hander

Finger tips 2cm from tip of pencil

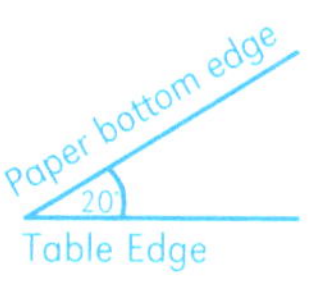

Chair slightly tilted

Full range of literacy activities

With this book, fully coordinated with the *Kindergarten Teacher's Guides* (Volume 1, Section 2), children learn to correctly and efficiently form the 26 lowercase and 26 uppercase letters while also building these related literacy skills:

- Phonemic awareness
- Strengthening letter/sound connections
- Blending sounds to read words
- Segmenting words to spell
- Sounds of digraphs: **th**, **sh**, **ch**, and **wh**
- Uppercase letter usage in names and sentences
- Spacing between words in sentences
- Punctuation of sentences

60+ Sight Words For further details, see page 3.

Teaching a new letter

To get the most from this book, coordinate its use with other Letterland materials.

Materials	Activities
Handwriting Songs CD *Handwriting Songs - Uppercase CD* *Living ABC* software	Display a very large letter on the board or use the *Living ABC* software version of the Handwriting Song. Children use large, full-arm movements to 'air-trace' the letter as they sing.
A-Z Copymasters	Children first trace the 'hollow letter' with their finger and then 'rainbow-write' (repeatedly write the letter with different colors).

Each time children start a new letter, you will want to make sure that they do the following:

- Start the letter in the correct place. (Dots indicate the start in 'hollow' letters.)
- Make strokes in the correct direction and sequence (arrows provide guidance).
- Make most lowercase letters with one continuous movement without picking up the pencil (exceptions: **f**, **i**, **j**, **k**, **t**, **x**, and **y**).

Getting these essentials right from the start will help ensure neat and fluent writing for years to come.

Icon key - new letter pages

- **Sing** or say the handwriting verse.
- **Finger-trace** the hollow letter with your finger as you sing.
- **Write** the letter with your pencil inside the hollow letter.

Children then write the letter on guide lines: first with directional arrows, next with dotted letters, and then with a dot for the starting point. Finally, they make several letters on their own. Icons remind them to:

- **Say** the sound as you **Write** the letter (e.g. "/**c**/ /**c**/").
- As you finish a set of letters, look back at them and choose the best one. **Rate** it by putting a (+) above it. Then try to make another one just like it.

After following the same steps with the uppercase letter, children apply the sound to words. **It is important to name the pictures with the children to ensure they are saying the intended word aloud.** The icons guide them to:

- **Say** the pictured word.
- **Listen** to the word.
- **Write** the first letter in the word.

Icon key - Teaching a Tricky Word

Children will be able to spell most of the 60+ common Sight Words in this book using the Letterland phonics you will teach in the first half of Kindergarten, but 18 of these words have irregular spellings (e.g. **the**, **of**, **said**). Each of these are presented on a half page as a Tricky Word. Before children do the activities in the book, you may want to introduce the word first in this way:

- Write the Tricky Word on the board and say it. Use it in a sentence or two.
- Have children say the word several times and perhaps make up sentences orally.
- Have children listen for the sounds in the word and talk about which letters are not saying their usual sounds. Mark these 'tricky parts' with wavy lines above as they are shown in the Practice book.

Tricky Word page

Give children a blank 3″ x 5″ index card or a folded piece of paper. For the first few times, guide them through the '**Look-Say-Cover-Write-Check**' routine to practice the word. The icons remind them of the steps:

- **Look** at the word and study it as you **Say** it. When you are ready...
- **Cover** the word with a card and **Write** it.
- **Check** to see if you spelled it correctly and if so, make a check above it.

If a child misspells a word, they should put a line through it or and follow the steps again.

The children write the word to complete a sentence. Finally, they copy the sentence below that.

Blending sounds to read words

Children use the letters and sounds they have learned to read words guided by these icons:

- **Write** over the dotted letters.
- **Blend** the sounds using the Roller Coaster Trick to read the word.
- **Circle** the picture that matches the word.
- **Write** the word.

Segmenting words to spell

Children segment the pictured word to spell it with letters and sounds they have learned. **It is important to say the pictured words with the children.** They then follow these icons:

- **Segment** the sounds in the word using the Rubber Band Trick.
- **Write** the letters that match those sounds.

vet

More activities

Additional activities include many letters, digraphs, words and sentences to write. Sentences are illustrated to enhance the meaning and many are related to stories children read in the *Phonics Readers*. When writing sentences, show children how they can use the finger on their other hand to leave a finger space between words. Have children read their page to a friend when finished.

See lots more suggestions for handwriting in the lessons and the Appendix of your *Teacher's Guide*.

Cc – Clever Cat

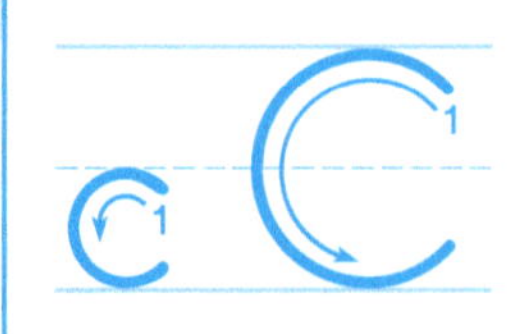

IMPORTANT Please refer to the **Icon Key**, page 2 to ensure you fully understand how to complete each activity and get the most from your handwriting book.

Sing – Finger-trace – Write

Say – Write – Rate

c

C

Say – Listen – Write

cat

up

ar

Ăă – Annie Apple

Say
Write
Say
Listen
Write
ake
pple
Mr. A
Say
Write
Say
Listen
Write
pron
corn

Dd – Dippy Duck

Hh – Harry Hat Man

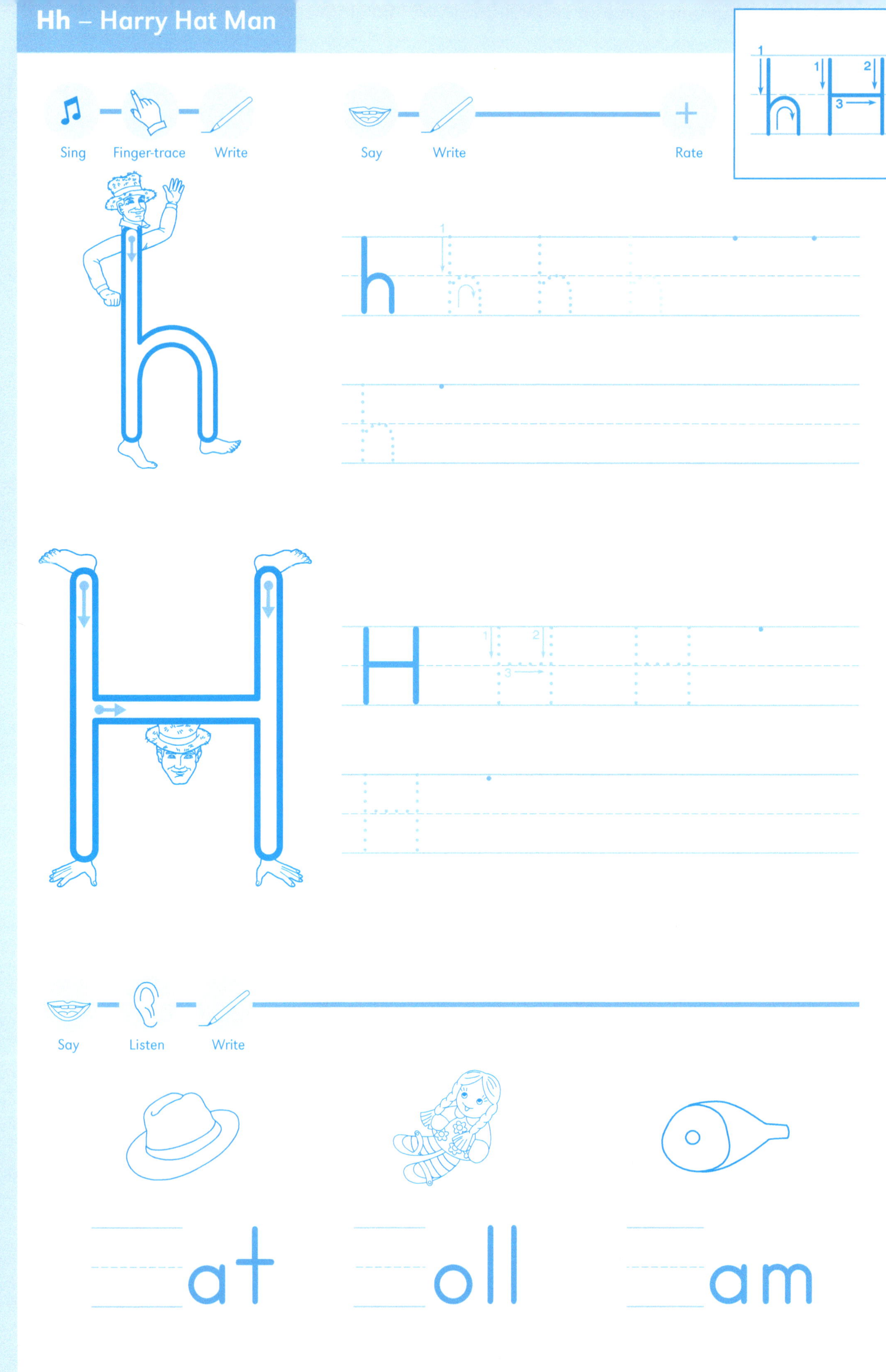

Say
Write
Say
Listen
Write
og
orse
and
uck
ill
eer
Write

Mm – Munching Mike

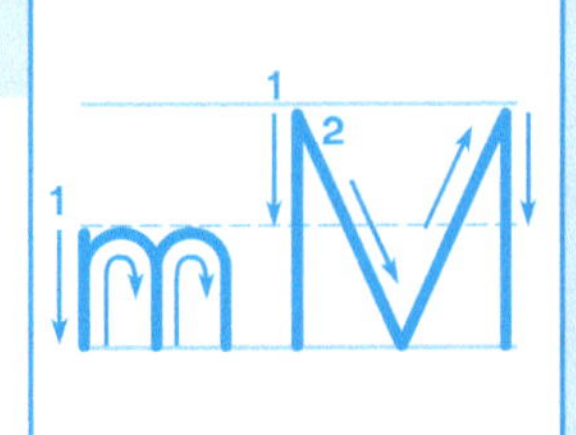

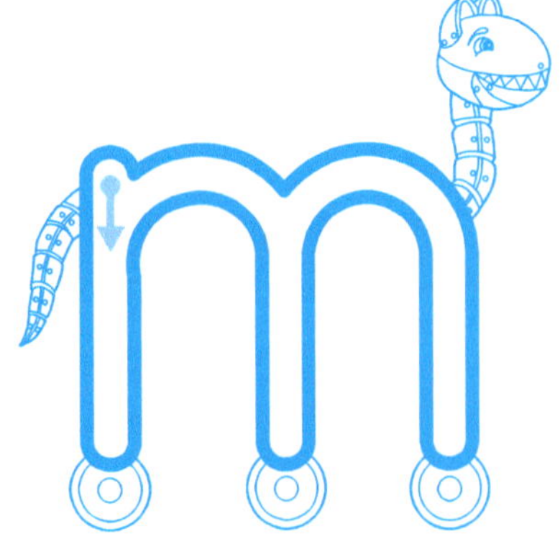

m

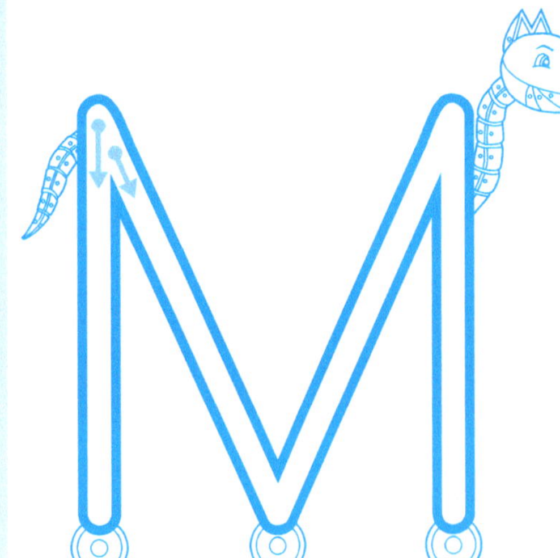

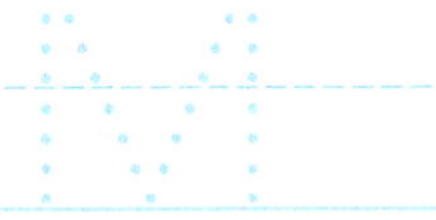

___ilk ___an ___en

Sing
Finger-trace
Write
Say
Write
Rate
Say
Listen
Write
ent
x
ie

Say
Write
m
t
M
T
Write
blend
Blend
Circle
Write
mat
ham
hat
Read
Write
mad Dad
cat mat

Sing
Finger-trace
Write
Say
Write
Rate
s
S
s
S
Say
Listen
Write
un
ock
ip

s/z/ – Sleepy Sammy

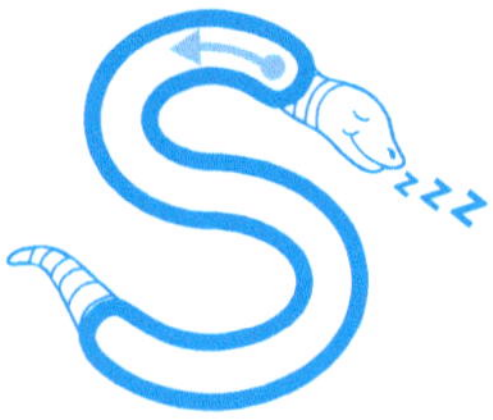

Say – Write

Say

Listen

Write

Circle

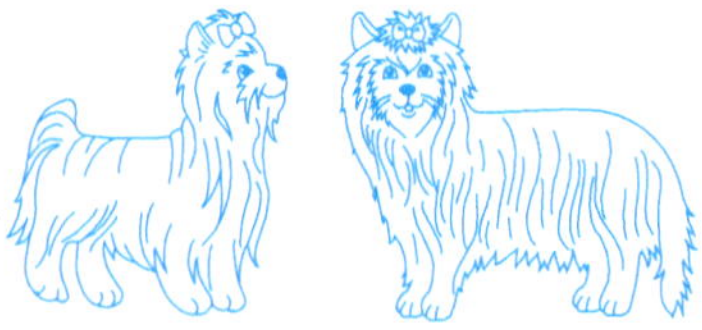

dog

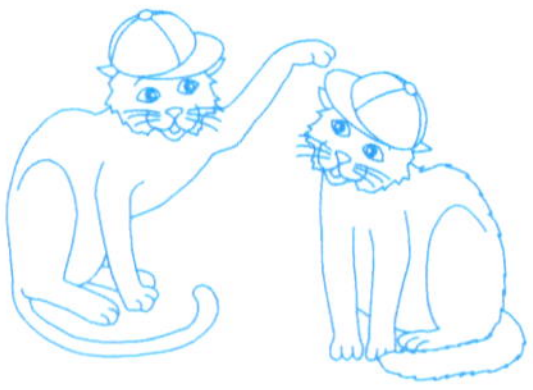

cat

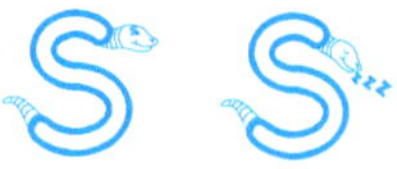

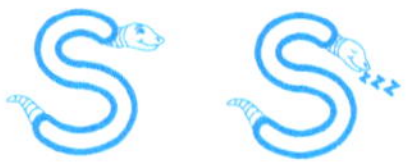

Tricky Word

Look – Say – Cover – Write – Check

Read – Write

Sam had a hat.

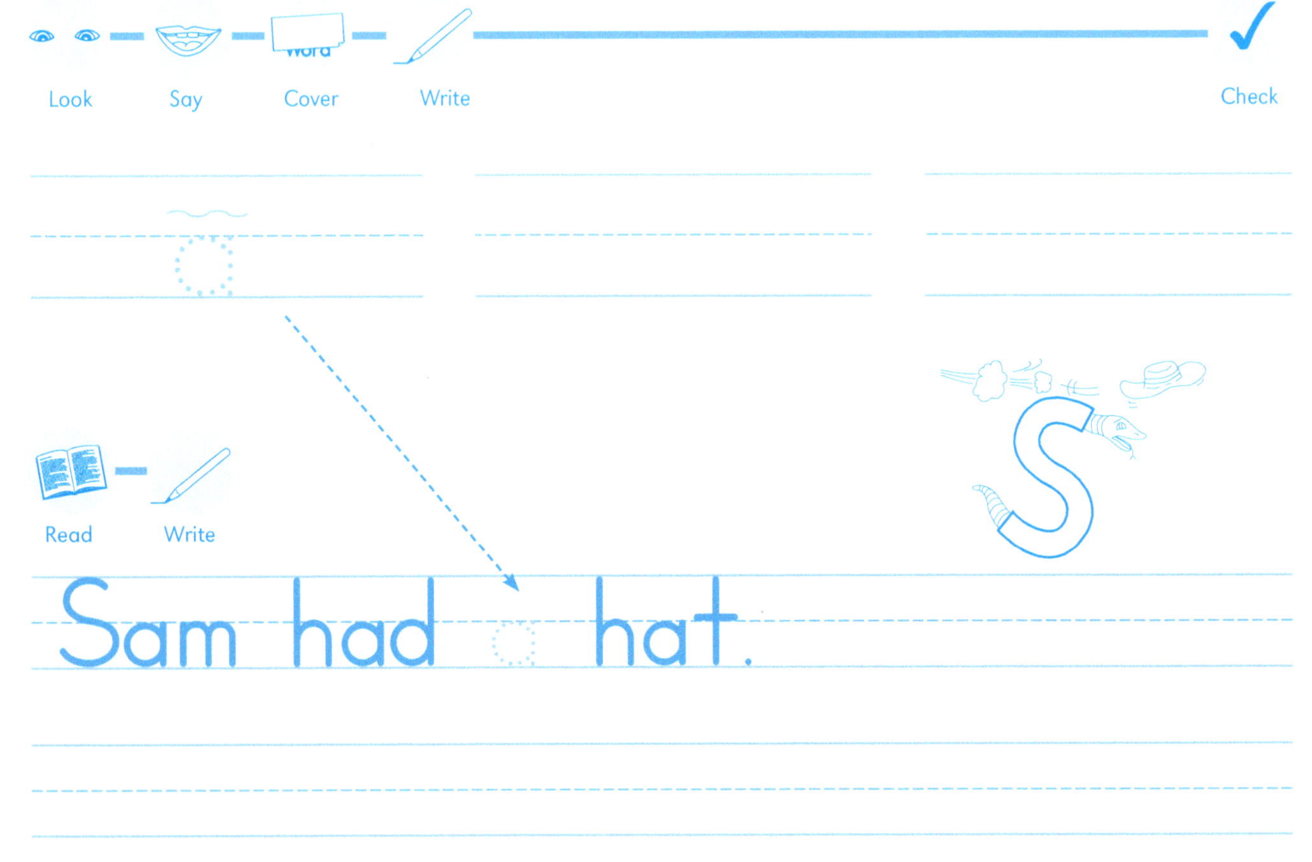

Sing
Finger-trace
Write
Say
Write
Rate
1
2
3
i
I
Say
Listen
Write
nk
tch
tar

Īi – Mr. I

Finger-trace – Say

Say – Write – Check

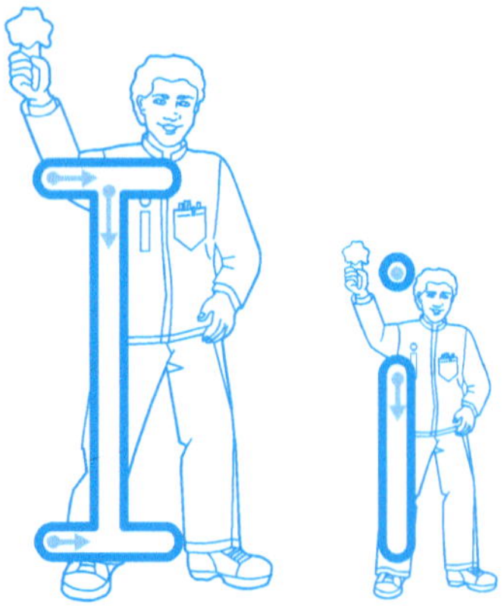

Read

Hi, I am Mr. I.

Write

Tricky Word

Look – Say – Cover – Write – Check

said

Read – Write

Nat said, "I hit it."

Nn – Noisy Nick

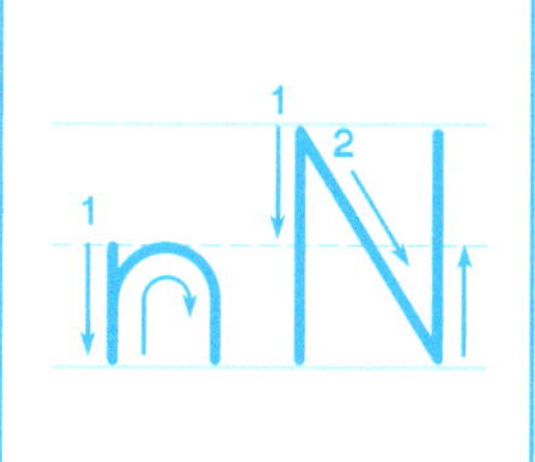

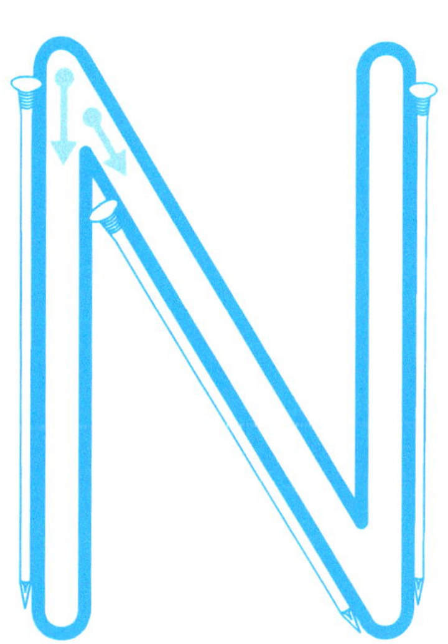

et

Say
Write
s
i
n
S
I
N
segment
Segment
Write
Word Bank
hit sad cats sit tan man
Read
Write
Did Nat sit and tan?

Sing
Finger-trace
Write
Say
Write
Rate
1
1
2
g
G
2
GO
G
G
Say
Listen
Write
oat
ail
o

Ŏŏ – Oscar Orange

Sing – Finger-trace – Write

Say – Write – Rate

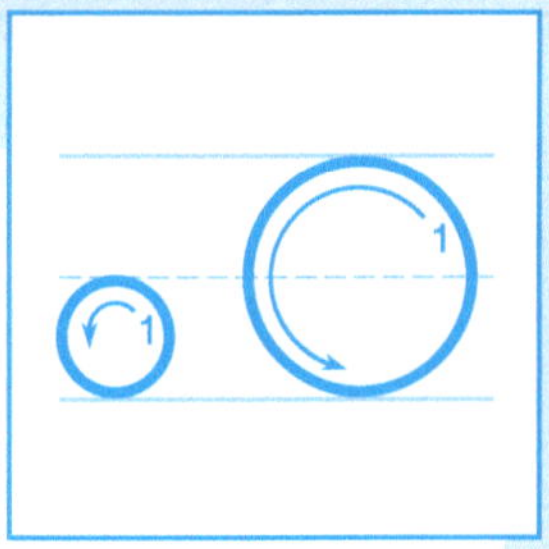

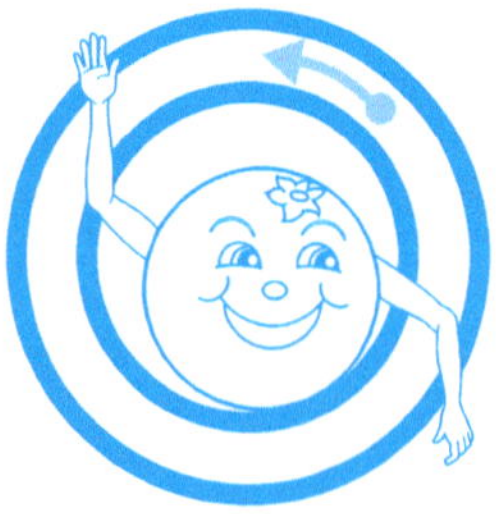

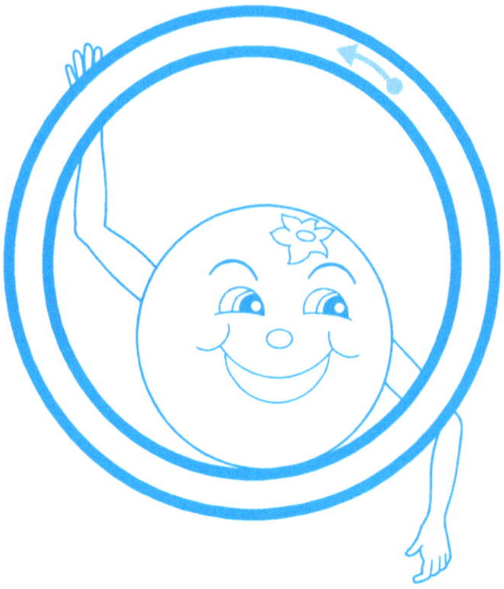

Say – Listen – Write

___n ___ff ___ame

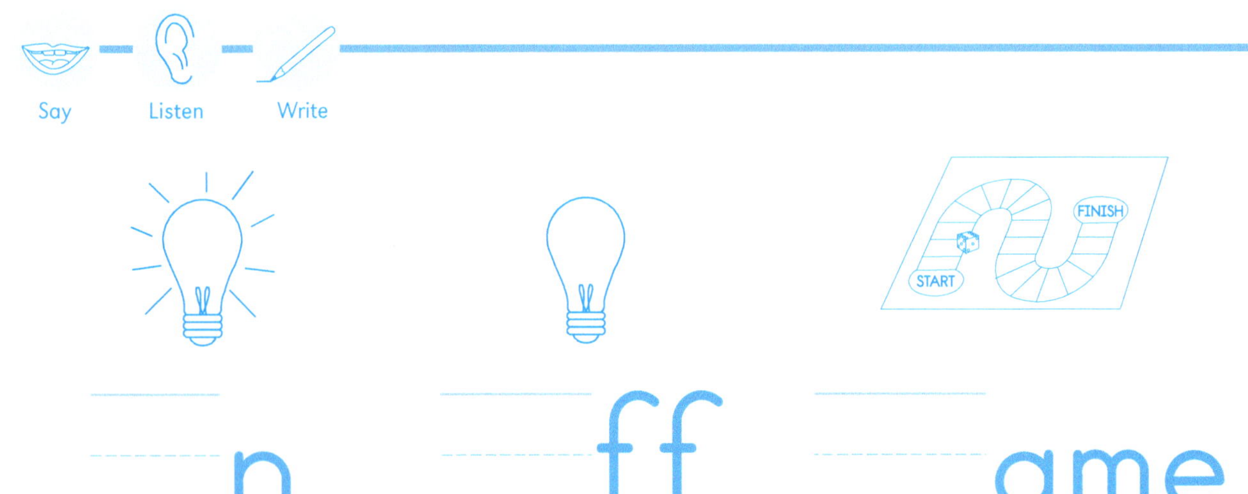

Say
Write
Check
Say
Listen
Write
OPEN
CLOSED
cean
pen
losed
Read
Write
Can it go?

Pp – Peter Puppy

Say
Write
Segment
Write
Word Bank
pop tan dig dog pin
Read
Write
p
p
Go, go! Oh, no! Pop!

Ĕĕ – Eddy Elephant

* Note: This letter shape can be formed in more than one way. The song words differ slightly from the formation shown here.

Finger-trace
Say
Say
Write
Check
Read
got
a hat!
Write
Tricky Word
Look
Say
Cover
Write
Check
Read
Write
pig is not in
pen.

Ŭŭ – Uppy Umbrella

Sing – Finger-trace – Write

Say – Write – Rate

u

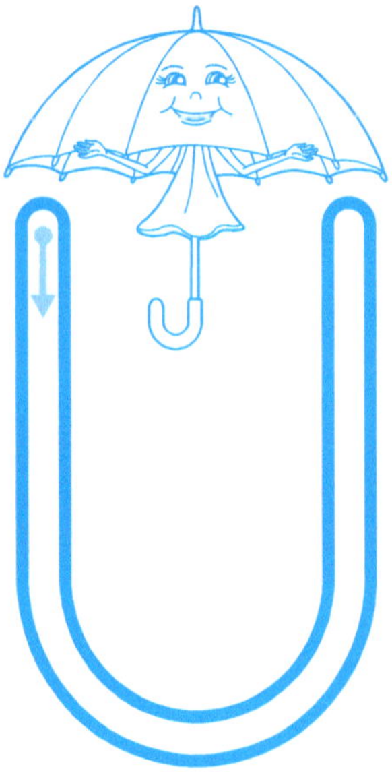

U *

Say – Listen – Write

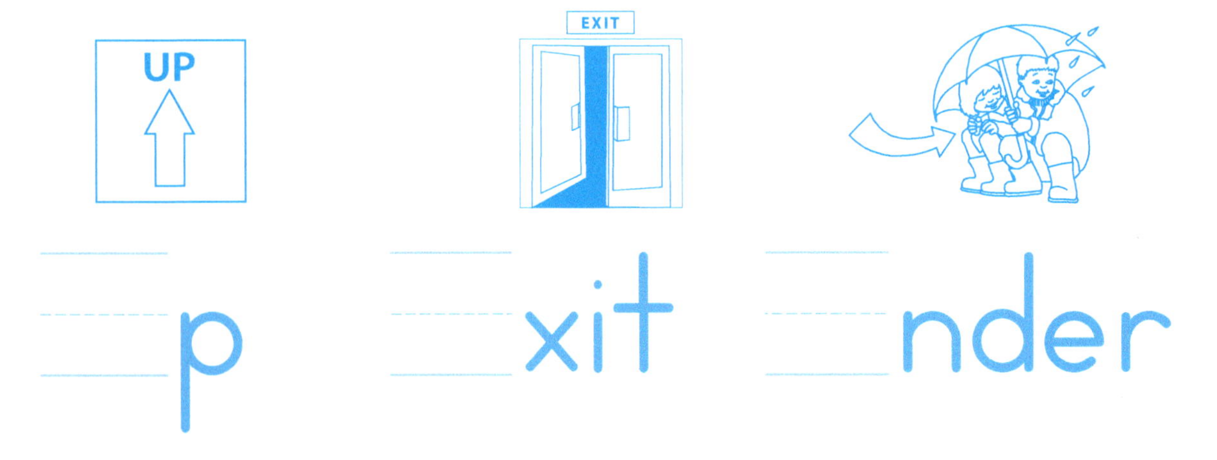

__p __xit __nder

* Note: This letter shape can be formed in more than one way. The song words differ slightly from the formation shown here.

Finger-trace Say

Say Write Check

nicorn

niform

Tricky Word

Look Say Cover Write Check

Read Write

He goes up get the nuts.

Kk – Kicking King

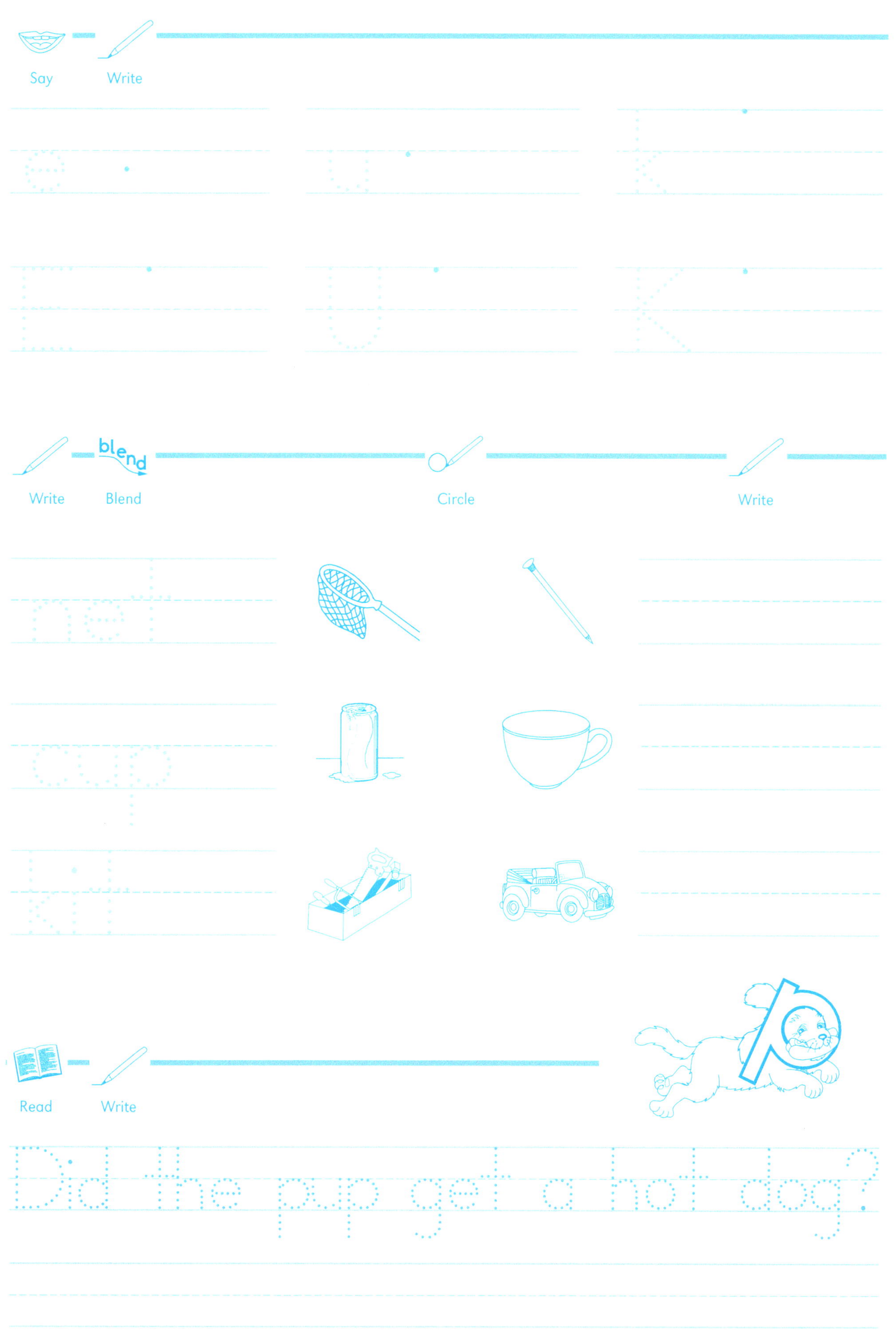
Say
Write
e
u
k
E
U
K
Write
blend
Blend
Circle
Write
net
cup
kit
Read
Write
Did the pup get a hot dog?

Digraph: ck

ck

Say Write

ck

Segment Write

Word Bank

sock sick dock duck neck nest

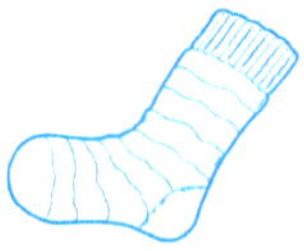

Tricky Word

Look Say Cover Write Check

see

Read Write

I Nick. I his socks.

ng

Say Write

ng

Write Blend Circle Write

sing

king

Tricky Word

Look Say Cover Write Check

like

Read Write

We ______ to sing a song.

Word Bank

ships shop She

I got Shep at the pet ________.

She likes to see the ________.

________ likes to nap. Hush!

ch

Say — Write

ch

Segment — Write

Word Bank

chap chick chop chin chip

th
Say
Write
Read
Write
This is Shep and me.
She naps in that shed.
Then she did this. No!
th
Say
Write
Read
Write
thick
thin

Say Write

ck ng sh

ch th

Write Blend Circle Write

sing

path

dish

Read Write

He checks on the chicks.

Sing
Finger-trace
Write
Say
Write
Rate
1
1
2
Say
Listen
Write
og
ing
ion

Ff – Firefighter Fred

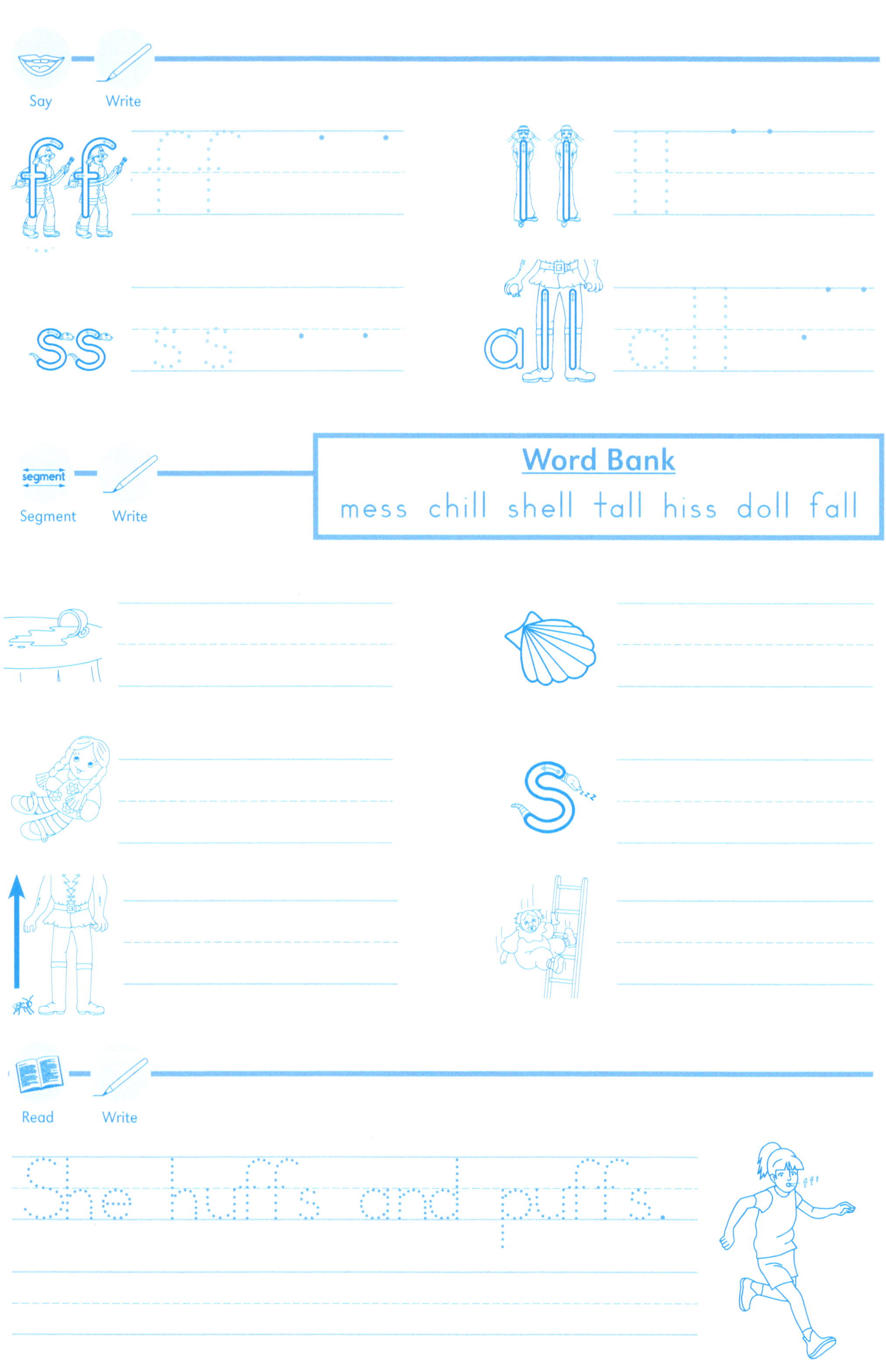

Say Write

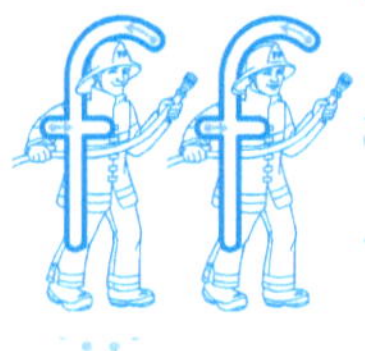

ff

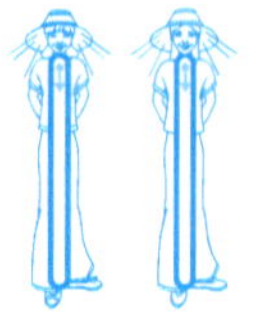

ll

ss

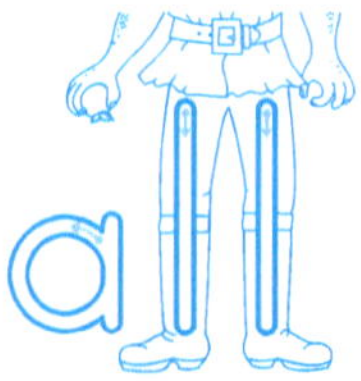

all

Segment Write

Word Bank

mess chill shell tall hiss doll fall

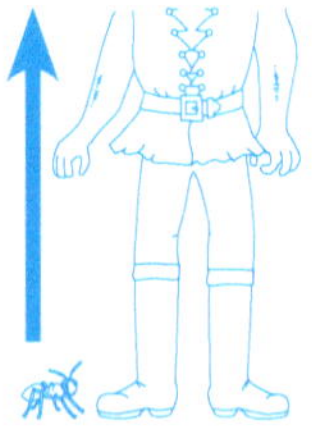

Read Write

She huffs and puffs.

Sing
Finger-trace
Write
Say
Write
Rate
b B
Say
Listen
Write
oat
ook
ox

Review: l, f, b

Finger-trace — Say — Say — Write — Rate

l f b

L F B

Segment — Write

Word Bank

bug leg lock bad

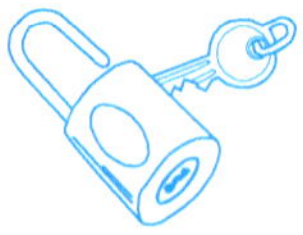

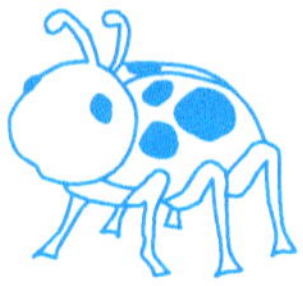

Tricky Word

Look — Say — Cover — Write — Check

of

Read — Write

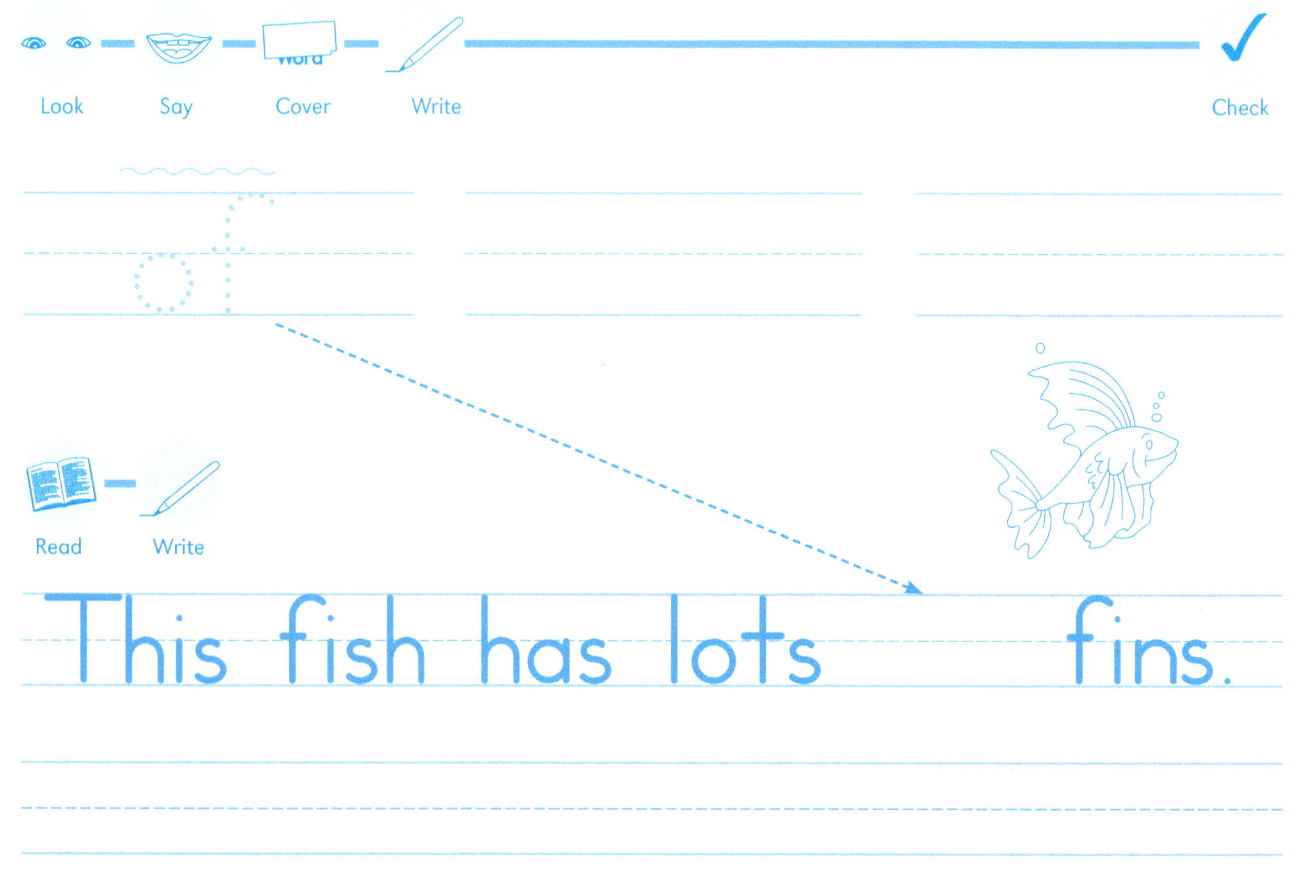

This fish has lots fins.

Jj – Jumping Jim

Rr – Red Robot

Qq – Quarrelsome Queen

Sing – Finger-trace – Write

Say – Write – Rate

Say – Listen – Write

___an

___ase

___am

ve
Say
Write
Read
Write
Mom gives him a bib.
Tricky Word
Look
Say
Cover
Word
Write
Check
for
Read
Write
Jim
I have a gift Jim.

o/ŭ/ – Bothersome Little Brother

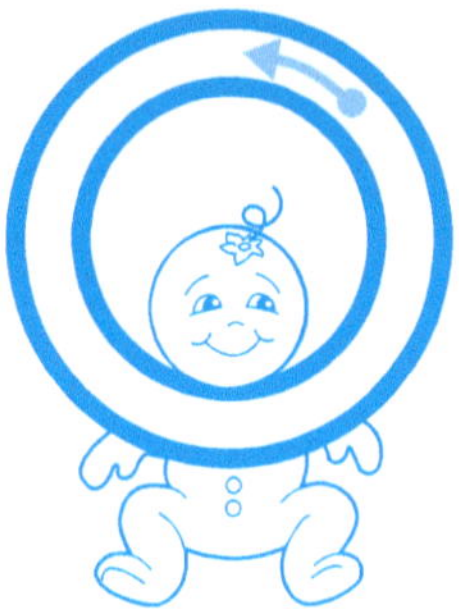

Say – Write – Rate

o

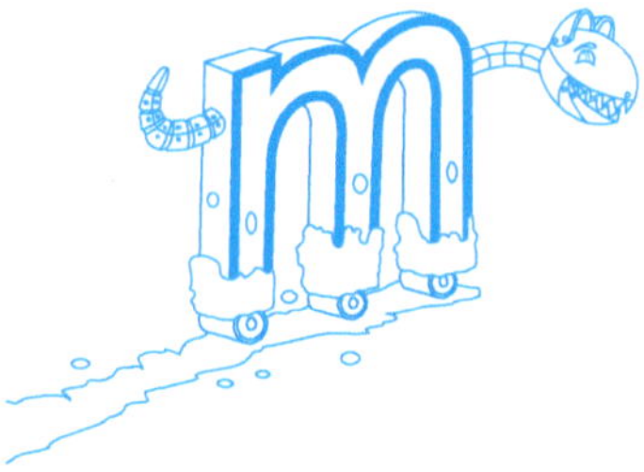

Read – Write

Come, have some fun!

Tricky Word

Look – Say – Cover – Write – Check

her

Read – Write

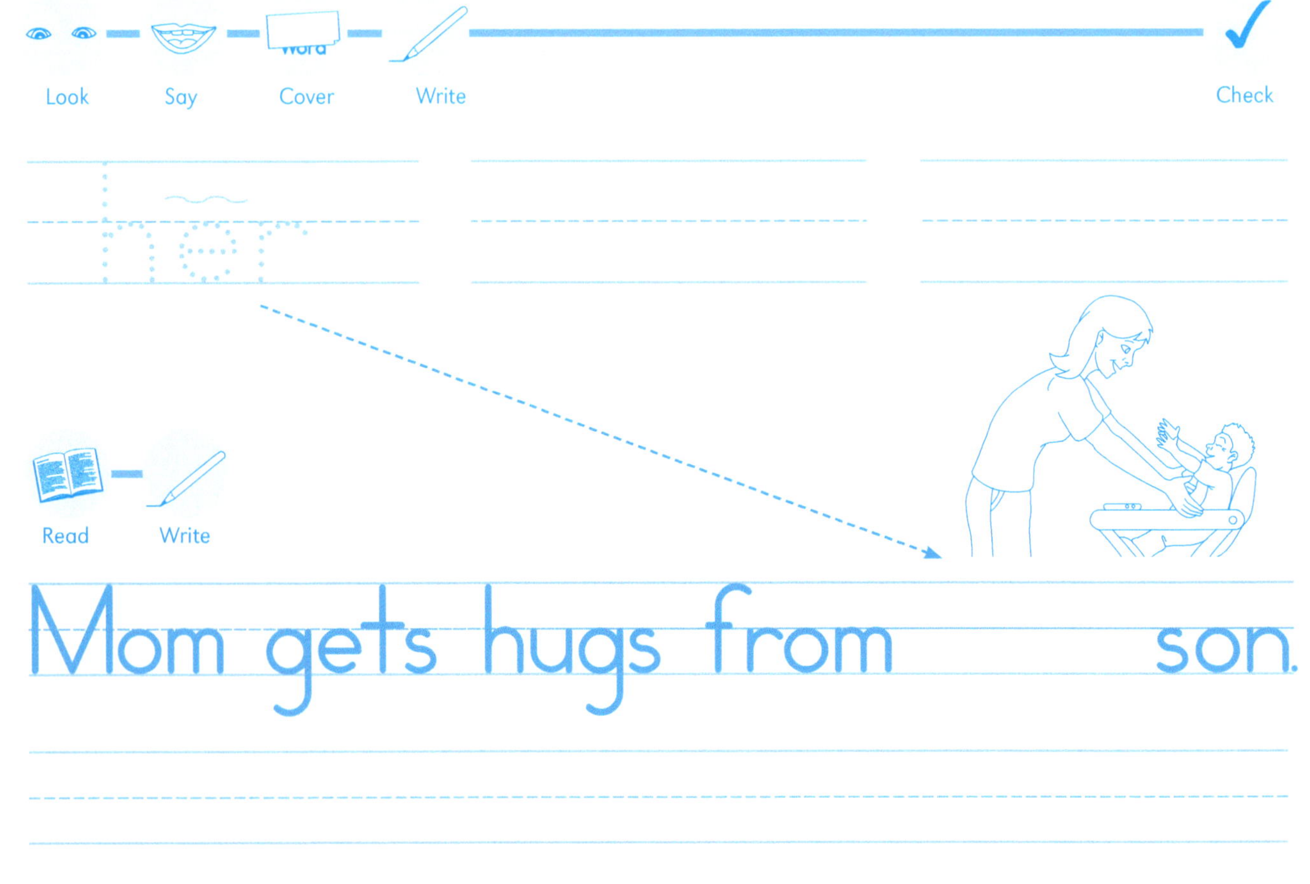

Mom gets hugs from son.

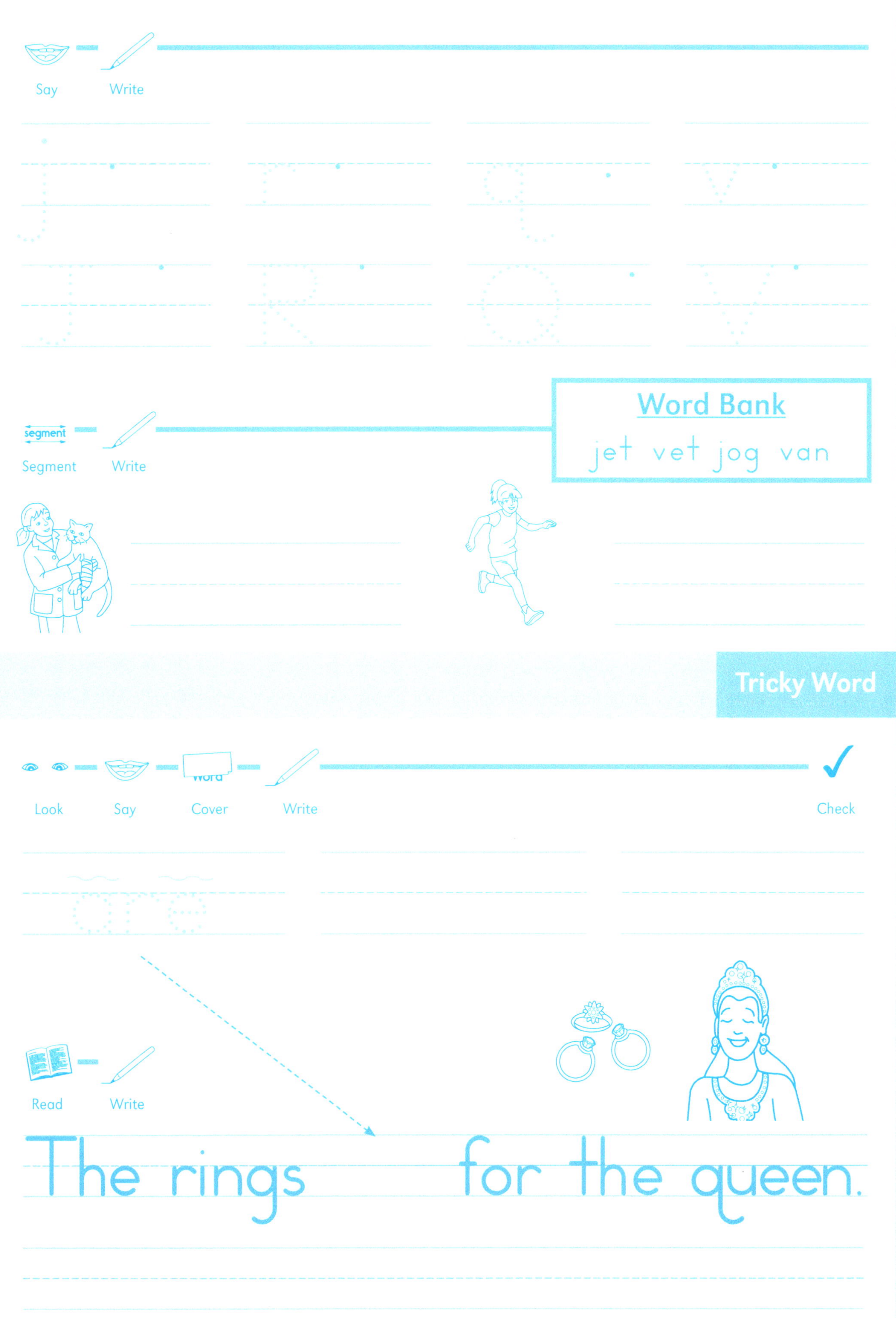
Say
Write
Segment
Write
Word Bank
jet vet jog van
Tricky Word
Look
Say
Cover
Write
Check
Read
Write
The rings for the queen.

Sing – Finger-trace – Write

Say – Write – Rate

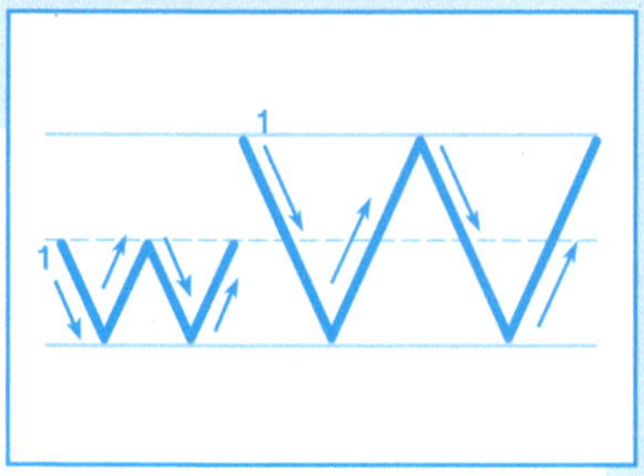

w

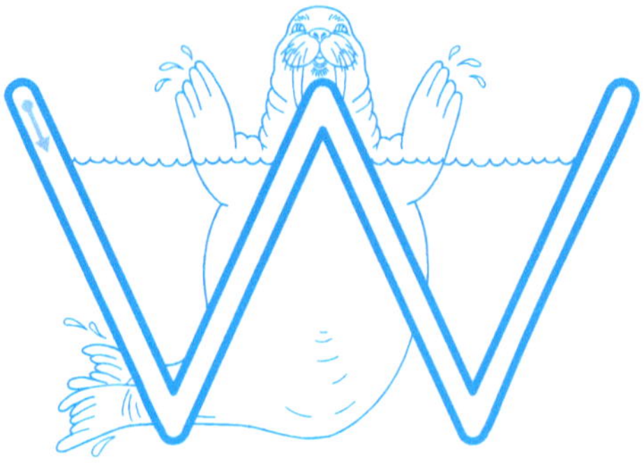

W

Say – Listen – Write

ing

atch

an

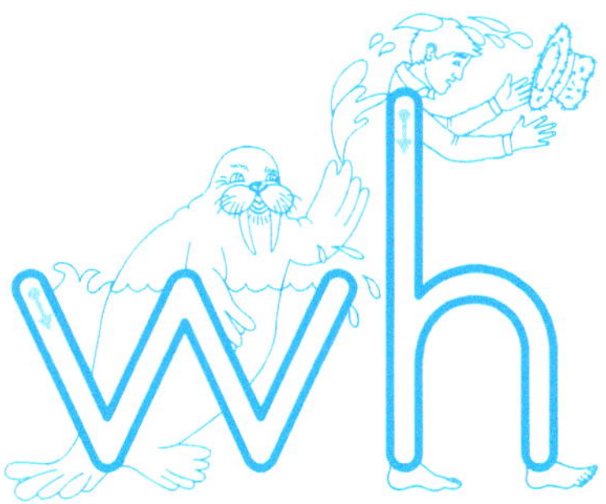

wh

Say – Write

wh

Segment – Write

when

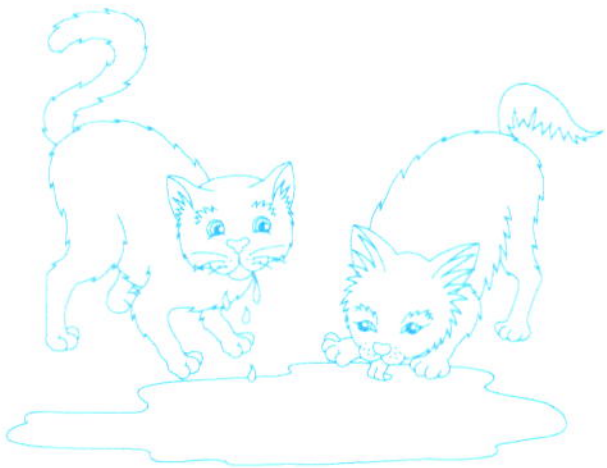

Which one is a dog?

Tricky Word

Look – Say – Cover – Write – Check

what

Read – Write

W is this long thing?

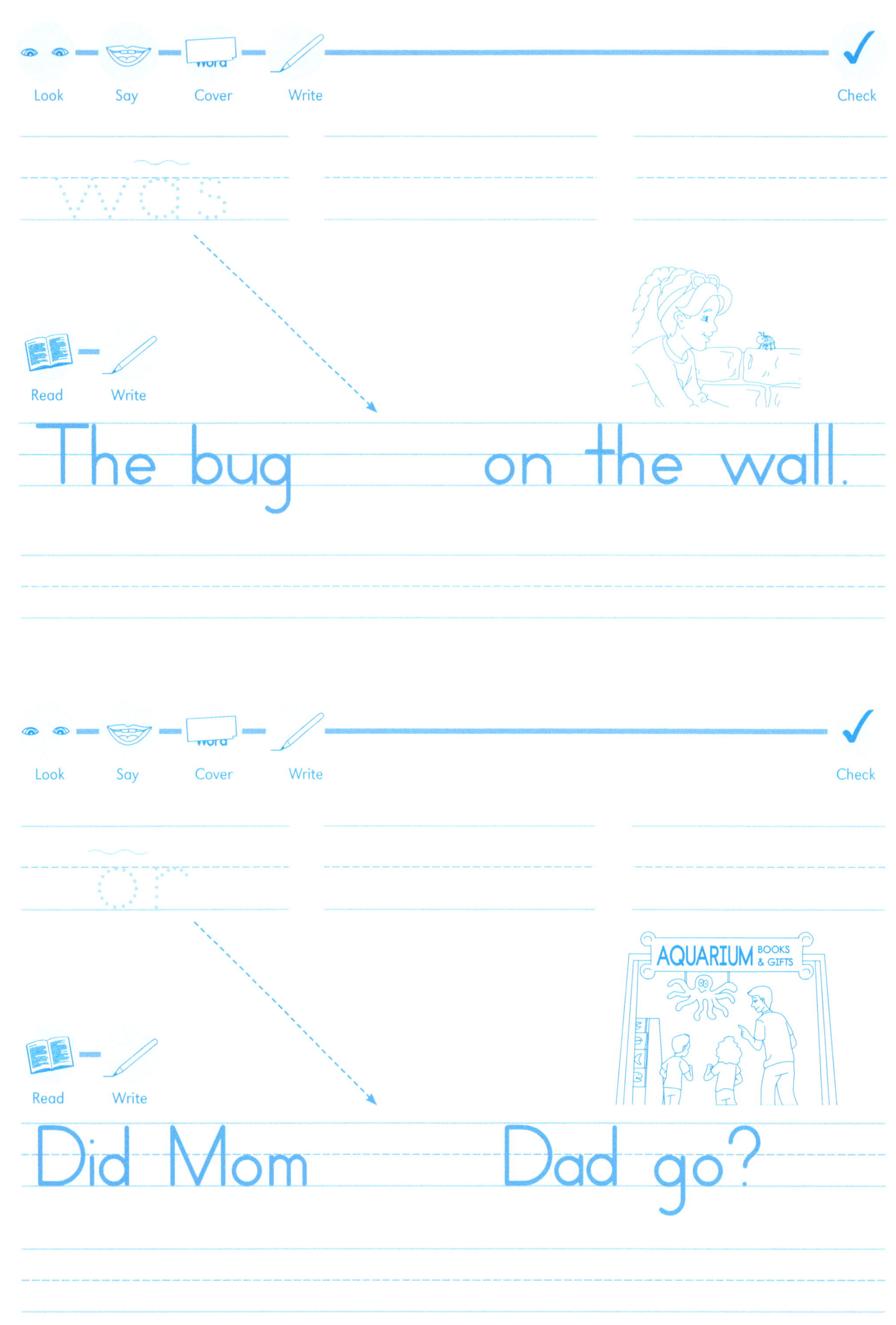
Look
Say
Cover
Write
Check
was
Read
Write
The bug on the wall.
Look
Say
Cover
Write
Check
or
Read
Write
AQUARIUM BOOKS & GIFTS
Did Mom Dad go?

Ma atch fo

Yy – Yellow Yo-yo Man

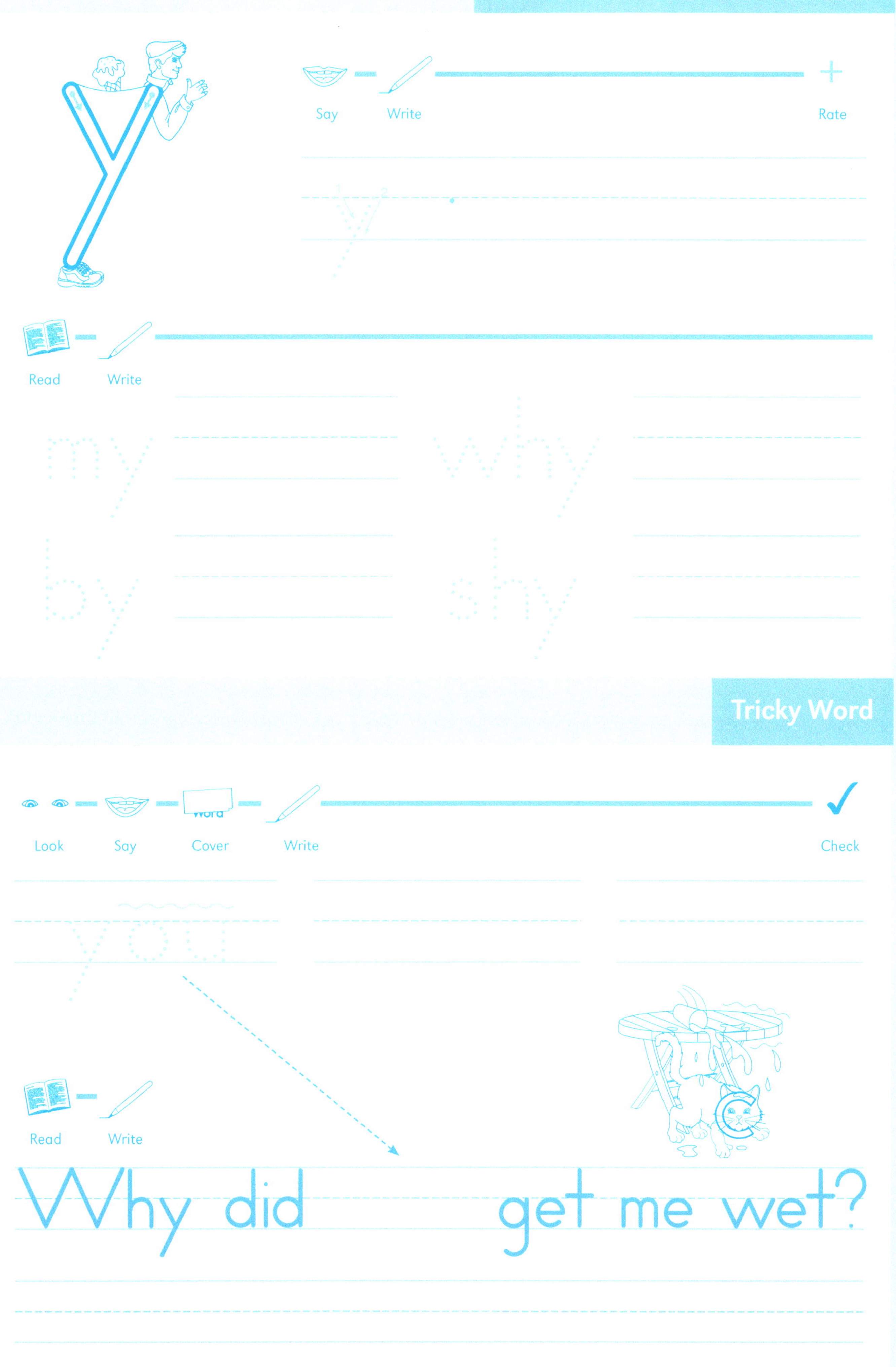
Say
Write
Rate
y
Read
Write
my
why
by
shy
Tricky Word
Look
Say
Cover
Write
Check
you
Read
Write
Why did get me wet?

Zz – Zig Zag Zebra

Sing – Finger-trace – Write

Say – Write – Rate

1 z 1 Z

z

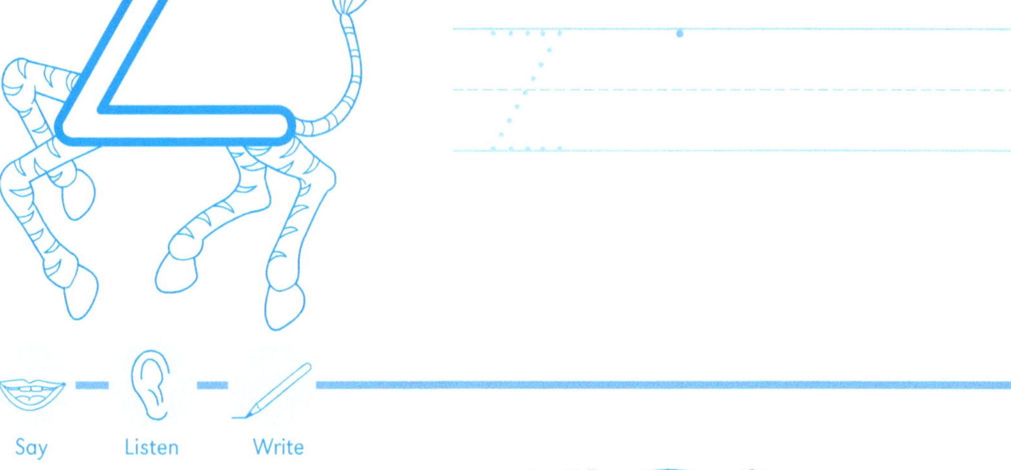

Z

Say – Listen – Write

__ebra __oo __awn

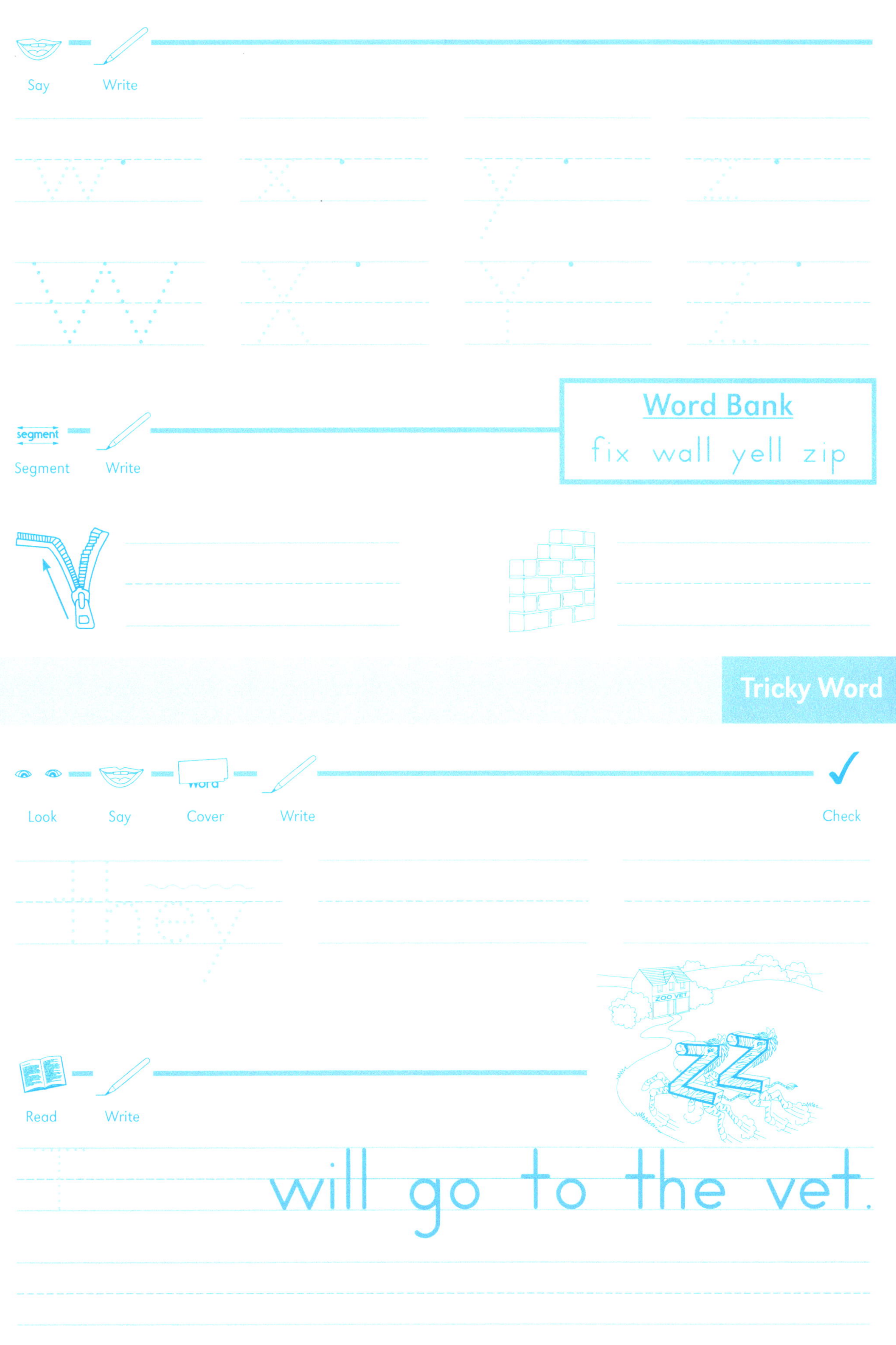

Say Write

Segment Write

Word Bank
fix wall yell zip

Tricky Word

Look Say Cover Write Check

Read Write

will go to the vet.

Look
Say
Cover
Write
Check
were
Read
Write
We fishing for crabs.
Look
Say
Cover
Write
Check
your
Read
Write
This is cake, Zack.
Happy
Birthday
ZACK